ADVENTURES IN THE SPIRIT

A Series of Prophetic Visions

Second Edition

BY RICHARD L SPANGLER

DEDICATION

To the Glory of God and to all those you seek to know Him and to learn who they are in Christ and to my wife Dorthy and my two beautiful daughters Mary and Sarah.

THANK YOU

Gene Markland and Michael Plemmons thank you for all your support and encouragement the writing of this book. You guys are a blessing.

A SPECIAL THANK YOU

Amy Bales your cover and illustrations are fantastic.

Table of Contents

Introduction

This book is a series of prophetic visions given to me by the Lord Jesus Christ over a six-month period. This series of visions has been an amazing experience for me. Receiving visions is a very biblical experience. The prophets Ezekiel, Isaiah, Daniel, and others had these experiences in the Old Testament. In the New Testament, the Apostles Peter, John, and Paul had prophetic visions and experiences, including being taken up into Heaven in some cases.

I want to make one thing clear; I did not seek out or try to force these visions and experiences to happen. There is no biblical basis for forcing these things to happen. Godly visions and experiences are given by God, for His purposes, and he gives them to whomever He chooses.

Anything else is dangerous; at the very least it is soulish in nature and at the worst a demonic deception.

I endeavor to walk with God to love him, and to know Him intimately. I spend time with Him in prayer and just wait and listen to hear what He has said. These are the keys, loving and seeking a relationship with God first. Then God will reveal to you what He wants to show to you. God desires a relationship with you and wants to reveal himself to you.

1

Introduction

But we all get so busy that we forget to say, "O.K. God I am here just to love on you and spend time with you." When we do that, we change; it is almost automatic. Our attitudes change in how we deal with stuff and people. Whatever the issue that is happening in your life, it doesn't seem as important as it did, because you are in the presence of God. When I am caught up in His presence, the cable bill doesn't seem to matter as much. What's for dinner doesn't appear to matter. Physical problems don't matter. The struggles of life don't matter, for you are in a place where you are loving God, and He is loving you. Our little bit of love we give Him gets overwhelmed by His love for us.

Jesus says, "To love God with all your heart, all your soul and all of your mind."

We think of the heart as the spirit, and the soul is a place of the emotions and the mind, it is a place of your will. In other words, you are to love God with all that you are. It is an act of your will; it is your choice to spend time with and to love God. Concentrate on loving God with everything you are and with everything you do. The fact is that loving God is the key to everything in God.

Introduction

The devil knows this. Also, he knows that if we declare God's Word without knowing the Lord personally, in an intimate, loving relationship, that he (the devil) can just keep on attacking us. Not having an intimate relationship is why many believers continue to come under attack, even when they declare the Word of God over their lives.

When we realize we need a closer relationship with the Lord, and decide to go for it with God, the devil uses life to distract us. There are television, computers, cell phone, and finances to distract us. Then devil stirs up our desire for more.

The distractions happened in my life when my two daughters were young, and there was always a need for extra money. I started working a second job. I would go to work on my full-time job at 5:30 a.m. get off at 2 p.m. and the second job by 3 p.m. and work to 10 or 11 p.m.

I didn't leave much time for a relationship with the Lord, or so I thought. I did have breaks and down times while working but, I did not use them to build a relationship with God. When I was not working, it was family time or time for church or time for me (mostly sleeping).

Introduction

I was ignorantly happy, but Father God wasn't. He remembered my commitment to love him and to know him more. Then, it started. The Holy Spirit would wake me up at 1 a.m. or 2 a.m., and I would spend an hour or two in the presence of God, experiencing his love and getting to know him. The time with God happened every night for almost two weeks. It was incredible spiritually, but physically I was exhausted.

I finally, said to the Lord, "I love spending time with you, but Lord why are waking me up in the middle of the night when you know my schedule?"

I heard the Lord say, "It's the only time I can spend time with you."

After that, I rearranged my schedule. I used my breaks and down times on my jobs to spend time with the Lord. Since that time, there have been no middle of night wake ups except to do intercession for someone and then after prayer, I can go right back to sleep and wake up refreshed in the morning.

Introduction

I learned that spending time with Father God and it is the first and best thing in my life. Loving the Lord and getting to know Him in an intimate relationship is amazing. Wherever I go, and whatever I am doing, I can be in the manifest presence of Father God. Choosing to be in the presence of God also hides you in His presence, He becomes your refuge.

The devil cannot come into the presence of God. In fact, he will flee (James 4:9). Being in God's presence means I that can hear His voice and see when He wants to use me to minister to someone. My wife says, "It isn't safe to take me anywhere because I almost always minister to someone."

Again, this comes from my willingness to Love and spend time with Him and build an intimate relationship. The good thing is that there is always more to learn and experience in God.

I pray these visions bless you and help you to love God and strengthen your relationship with the Lord. I hope these visions will help you to realize and know who you are in Christ.

God Bless you,

Richard

THE WARRIOR

THE WARRIOR

I keep seeing a vision of myself in the full armor of God. The armor of silver. On the Breastplate, there is a roaring lion on it. As I look at the Shield, there is the same roaring lion on it. On the handle of the sword, there is the head of a roaring lion. As I look to the left and the right, there are many in the same uniform and with the same symbol on their armor, their shields, swords, breastplates, and helmets glowing with the Glory of God.

In the distance, I see an army moving away in full retreat. Looking down at my feet, I see there are bodies of the demonic laying there and at the feet of the Army of God. The bodies of the demons stretch as far as the eyes can see.

I do not remember the battle, just the roaring of praise and worship and the Glory of God falling, then the piles of the enemies of God, the Lord of Hosts.

We all worship and praise Him and as we do the Glory of God falls again. This time, as the Glory lifts, all the bodies are gone; there is no sign of a battle.

THE WARRIOR

Instead of a battlefield, we are in the field, but it transformed into a beautiful place of rest, a green pasture with the River of God flowing through it. There are flowers of every type and color everywhere. The aroma of the flowers is amazing and overwhelms my senses. They seem to glow with the Glory of God. There are numerous fruit-bearing trees, with each tree having its type of ripe fruit.

I pick what looks like an apple from one of the trees and bite into it. There is an explosion of wonderful flavor in my mouth; it tastes like nothing I have ever tasted before. Upon eating it, new strength flows into my body.

Some of the army, like me, were enjoying the fruit; others were wading and playing in the river. Still, others were squeezing what looked like oranges and putting the juice (which looked more like oil) into bottles. We all enjoy this time of rest. Though it seemed like days of refreshing, it had only been a few hours.

Then suddenly, I sensed the need to put the armor on again, and some others are doing the same.

THE WARRIOR

The shofars (a ram's horn trumpet blown by the ancient Hebrews in battle and during religious observances) blew, and everyone else put on their armor.

The army formed up and began to move forward; those of us felt the need to put on the armor before the shofars sounded are now in the lead.

Reaching the top of the next hill, we look down on the enemy's army. There is a lot of screaming and cursing at each other. They were blaming each other for the defeat they had suffered. There is an evil darkness that surrounds this army with everything around it dead or dying. The members of this army are so intent on their infighting that they have not noticed us on top the hill looking down on them. Then, shofars sound again, and we begin to worship, the Glory of God begins to fall again.

The army of demons, looking up the hill, screams louder. They cover their ears and run in every direction they could away from the Glory of God rolling down the hill into the valley. The glory cloud becomes so thick that we can no longer see or stand. As it lifts, we are again in a restored pasture land with the River of God flowing through it. This time we camp for the night.

THE WARRIOR

At my campfire, I see my friends, Mike, Gene, and Jean. It is great seeing them, but I am not surprised that they are there.

We have a splendid time enjoying each other's stories of our time with the Lord Father God and the battles, and the victories won in our lives. We all agree that there will always be battles and that there will always victory in Christ.

I look up and notice a beam of light just beyond the trees near where we are sitting. I get up and to go toward the light. Moving through the trees, I notice that the light is running along a line in each direction. As I move closer to the light, the reason for the light is evident. The watchmen are on guard and are praying. As they pray, the light of God's glory radiates from them and connects to the other watchmen. This connection creates a wall of God's glory around the camp.

Walking along the wall of glory, I can look and see some of the demonic forces peering at the wall of glory and trying to find a way to attack us. Occasionally, a fiery dart is coming in my direction, but it hits the wall of glory and disintegrates. I thank God for these watchmen, who stand guard by night in prayer and intercession.

THE WARRIOR

As I move between the watchmen's camps, I sense an evil presence. The wall of glory is not there. A watchman's camp should be, but it is not here.

I quickly draw my sword, and it gives off a powerful light revealing all that is hiding in the darkness. Demons are moving through the opening in the wall. I am suddenly in the middle of a battle, surrounded by evil. The darkness of the night makes this worse. The demons use the darkness as cover. Suddenly they charge out at me from the darkness. As I battle these evil beings, I begin to sing and worship the Lord.

The demons, up to now, have been quietly whispering to me their threats and condemnations, but as they hear me worship, they forget themselves and yell at me to stop worshipping. The demons' yelling alerts the army, and soon they find themselves overwhelmed. The demons are in full retreat as the wall of glory is restored. There are many in the Army of God that pick up the calling to be watchmen in this place. I thank them and continue my rounds.

I stop at each watch camp and pray for and encourage each watchman in their duties.

THE WARRIOR

Encouraging and praying for them, causes them to pray even more which increases the wall of God's glory. Thus, protecting the camp of the army of the Lord.I make way back to the camp, and make a mental note to encourage these prayer warriors when the Lord brings them across my path.

The next day the army is once again moving, to another battle and another victory. After the fight, we come across some others from another fight. They are weary, and some are injured. I wonder how they were injured. For the battles, we have fought complete victories with no one even getting a scratch. Thank you, Lord.

We stop and minister to them. It was beautiful to watch as those, who had bottles of oil from the orange- like fruit, poured the oil onto the wounds and pray the wounds heal. Others of us shared the fruit with them to strengthen them. The army had to move on, so some of our group stayed and tended to those recovering from their wounds.

There were some from this group wanted to come with us and did. I had an uneasy feeling that they were not ready, but they came anyway.

THE WARRIOR

We came upon the enemy again. This time the battle was more intense. We even found ourselves in hand to hand combat. The army of evil seemed more determined than ever not to suffer another defeat. Their screams, at times, were deafening and the force of their attack was furious.

Some of those who came with us broke ranks and ran. I do not feel anger towards them, but only sadness that they will not see the victory that is sure to come.

One of the demons grabs my left arm, the one holding the Shield of Faith. This demon radiated evil and hatred all around him. Evil and hate distorted his face, his eyes were black as pitch, and there was no light in them at all. He violently shook me and yelled at me to drop the shield. The demon's breath smells like 100 rotten eggs (if evil can smell). Finally, he began just started screaming at me. The noise was deafening. The demon screamed out all my past sins, condemnations, and my unworthiness. Amid this, I remember, 1 John 1:9 (NIV) which says, "if we confess our sins, he is faithful and just and will forgive us our sins and purify us from all unrighteousness."

THE WARRIOR

I take note that this demon takes care not to touch the Shield of Faith, even while shaking me and screaming at me. I also noticed that all he was doing was screaming, cursing and shaking me. He had no weapons that I could see, and his scream was all the power he had. I looked around and saw it was the same everywhere on the battlefield. The demons were doing a lot of screaming at us to drop our Shields of Faith, but they had no weapons. But, when one of us drops our shield, the demons were on top of him, beating him unmercifully with their fists.

It is then that I realized how those we helped earlier became injured. Again, the demons had no actual weapons. It is then; I remember Colossians 2:15 (NIV) which says, "And having disarmed the powers and authorities, he made a public spectacle of them, triumphing over them by the cross."

In other words, the demons had no real power. Even the fiery darts had no effect if we kept our faith. I also realized that we are in Christ and He is in us, and we have all that Christ is within us. I realize that we have His authority and His power. All we must do is to use the Power of God in us.

THE WARRIOR

At this point, I have had enough. Somehow, I manage to swing the Sword of the Spirit around and cut off the demon's arm. It runs away screaming in pain. The stench, (it was worse than the smell of a 1000 sewage treatment plants) from demonic arm was horrible and gut wrenching. Then, with the others, I quickly move to help those who were being beaten by the demons. We use the Sword of the Spirit, wheeling it with power and faith. When we strike some of the demons, they let go and run away holding their wounds and screaming in pain. Others fall to the ground, paralyzed, as if they were dead, as we push them away with the Shield of Faith. The battle turns, as one by one we begin to worship the Lord. Some stand and worship and soon others of us do the same. The demons scream for us to stop as they hold their ears and run away. Driving back the enemy with Worship, the Glory of God falls as before. The demons that were paralyzed and lay on the ground are swept away by the Glory of God. The battlefield is transformed again into a place of rest and refreshing. I think to myself, each battle is different, but the outcome is the same, VICTORY!!!Then I look at my left arm. The demonic hand that had gripped me was gone. It had been cleaned away by the Glory of God.

THE THRONE ROOM

THE THRONE ROOM

I am sitting on the river bank, still wearing the Armor of God, rejoicing and praising God for the day's victory. Suddenly, the Glory of God falls on me and lifts me up higher and higher until I find myself standing at the entrance to the Throne Room of God. The massive doors are open and looking up, the entry appears to be several miles high and glows with the Glory of God. I hear the voices of the Father, the Son and the Holy Spirit calling me to enter.

Entering the Throne Room, I am amazed and overwhelmed. Thousands of people are stretched out on the floor worshipping the Lord and crying out in intercession. I notice that some of those on the floor disappear and others appear to take their place. These appearances and disappearances are amazing. Those who finish their time of intercession before God go and those starting their intercession appear and take their place. They are in the spirit, just as I am in the spirit and yet I am still on earth and so are they. The natural mind can not comprehend the wonders of the throne room.

There are also thousands standing and worshiping God. The same thing is happening with them as with those in intercession.

THE THRONE ROOM

When they finished their time of worship, they disappear. Then others appear as they worship God.

The Holy Spirit is hovering over them. From time to time the Spirit comes down and touches one of the intercessors or one of the worshippers, and they begin to glow with the anointing of God. Sometimes the Holy Spirit comes down upon whole groups of intercessors and worshippers, and the light of the anointing is almost blinding.

Simultaneously, many angels are moving among and ministering to the intercessors and the worshippers. I stand in awe at the incredible beauty of this coming and going in the Throne Room of Heaven. Again, the voices of the Holy Spirit, Jesus, and the Father beckon me to the throne.

Moving closer to the throne among hundreds of thousands of angels, I notice some of the angels are in armor; seemingly waiting for orders. These angels are robust and powerful and are fierce looking. These are, without a doubt, warrior angels. There are also angels, who have a softer appearance. They disappear and reappear seconds later; I sense in my spirit; these angels are messengers.

THE THRONE ROOM

 Finally, there is another rank of angels, and all they do is worship. It is impossible for me to describe the sound of worship in the throne room.

 My strength is gone; I feel the power of the Holy Spirit, moving me forward. I am still wearing the Armor of God. I finally reach the throne and fall to my knees before the great Three in One, the Father, Son and the Holy Spirit, who are there but also everywhere.

 At the Throne of God, I see two great angels standing on each side. In front of each angel, there is a large open book. Also present is the Ark of the Covenant, on top of the ark, is the Mercy Seat covered with the blood of Christ. One of the angels lifts a page, looks at it, smiles. He removes the page from the book. When I say, "removes the page," I mean, it is like the page was never in the book. The angel then puts the removed page on top of the Mercy Seat, and it completely disappears in the blood of Christ. Once the page dissolves in the blood of Christ, an aroma rises. If love could have an aroma, then this would be it. The lovely aroma fills the throne room.

THE THRONE ROOM

I have smelled this aroma before. From time to time when in worship the manifest presence of God fills a place. But here the fragrance is pure and overwhelming.

The other angel writes something in the other book, and a roar of praise rises from outside the throne room. Every time one angel places a page from the book on the Mercy Seat and one angel writes in the other book, a roar of praise occurs. The pages placed on the Mercy Seat are the records of sins that are now gone forever because of the blood of Christ. In the other book, an angel writes the names in the Lamb's Book of Life. Sadly, not every page that the angel picks up is placed on the Mercy Seat. The Angel looks at them and then with a great sigh puts the pages back in the book. These are people that came to the point of decision and did not repent and did not accept Christ. I weep as my heart is breaking for the lost.

Father and Jesus step forward and pour anointing oil on my head. The oil runs down onto my shoulders, then over my whole body, covering me in oil.

THE THRONE ROOM

I hear the Father, Jesus and the Holy Spirit say in unison, "New Anointing, New Revelation, New Authority, New Power and New Strength are now upon you." They placed their hands on me, and I feel tremendous love and power flowing through me. At this moment the garment of Praise, which I wear under the Armor of God, begins to melt through my skin. There is no pain, but there is a warm feeling moving deeper and deeper into me. I feel praise flowing from inside of me. My heart is pumping praise and worship to God throughout my entire body.

The armor of God is also transforming from silver to gold. The armor is also melting and flowing over every inch of my body. The armor is a merging with my skin and becoming part of me; it is no longer separate from me; it is becoming my skin and reflecting the Glory of God. After what seems like hours, I am finally able to stand.

The Lord then speaks with a commanding voice and says, "GO FORTH IN VICTORY."

THE CAMPAIGN
BEGINS AGAIN

THE CAMPAIGN BEGINS AGAIN

I find myself in my tent in the camp of the Army of God. Everything changed (Even now as I type this I feel the change within me.) Stepping out of my tent I see, hundreds of others also wearing the Golden Armor of God, as they come out of their tents. It amazes me that so many of us have been changed yet it was as if I was the one only there.

We see the army of the evil one massing for a counterattack. I immediately gave commands to those wearing the Silver Armor of God. I give orders, and the shofars near me sound the call to battle. The others in God's Golden Armor are doing the same. Each one knows his part and the parts the others have, and giving instructions to those who are with us.

One of the men brings me a beautiful stallion. To say it was white would be an understatement; it was glowing white. On it was a beautiful golden saddle which is amazing to behold. I mount this beautiful animal as some of the others in the Golden Armor of God mount theirs. We move into position, behind the hills on either side of the enemy. Our forces are now on the right and left flanks while the other part of the Army of God is in front of the enemy.

THE CAMPAIGN BEGINS AGAIN

It was then that I realized the trap that the enemy had set for us had now become a trap for them! The shofars sounded the attack, and we ride to the tops of the hills the Golden Armor of God reflecting the sun.   Reaching the top of the hill, we worship as the Glory of God radiates out of the armor and flows down into the valley below.

The demons break ranks. Some run away, while others run forward toward the waiting Army of God.

The Army of God offers praise and worship, and the Glory of God becomes powerful and overwhelming. We continue in worship until the intensity of the Glory is so great that no one can see the man or woman beside him or her. As we finish worshipping, the glory begins to lift. In the valley below, there is not a demon in sight. Instead, the valley and the hillsides are radiating the Glory of God.

After the battle, the restoration of beauty is amazing. However, there was no time to enjoy it. The Holy Spirit urges us to press the attack on the enemy. We quickly formed up and moved out to pursue the enemy.

THE CAMPAIGN BEGINS AGAIN

As we moved forward, we meet no opposition. Everywhere we place our feet renewal, and the Glory of the Lord breaks out in the land.

We reach the top of a ridge and behold a massive army of evil below, stretching out as far as we see. This evil army is aware of us but in their pride, which I can sense have made no preparations to defend an attack by us. They know, they vastly outnumber us. This army reminds me of the army of the Midianites that Gideon faced. I also remembered Shamgar, a judge of Israel, who slew 600 with an ox goad (a pointy stick). Then scripture comes to mind, that one would put 1000 to flight and two 10,000.

Those of us on horseback pull out our two-edged swords that glow with the power of the Word of God. We charge towards the enemy camp and as we do our armor shines. The Lord's army that is on foot also charges forward, running towards the enemy.

They run and keep up with those of us on horses (The scripture, they shall run and not grow weary comes to mind). Their armor and swords glow with the Glory of God. At this point, the enemy camp falls into chaos.

THE CAMPAIGN BEGINS AGAIN

There are shouts of blame and curses. Some try to stand their ground. Other demons run away as fast as they can. We continue to praise and worship God as the Glory of His presence comes upon us. We charge into the enemy's camp and meet only a token resistance. The demons are busier attacking each other, than attacking us!

The Glory of God is getting thicker and heavier covering entire valley with the Glory of the Lord of Hosts. The battle is soon over. After a time of worship in the Father's Presence, the Glory of God lifts. We are in a beautiful valley with surrounding hills and a great river which flows through the valley.

We all enjoy the rest and peace and the resident Glory of God in the land. Suddenly, I am caught away by the Spirit.

THE WARROOM OF HEAVEN

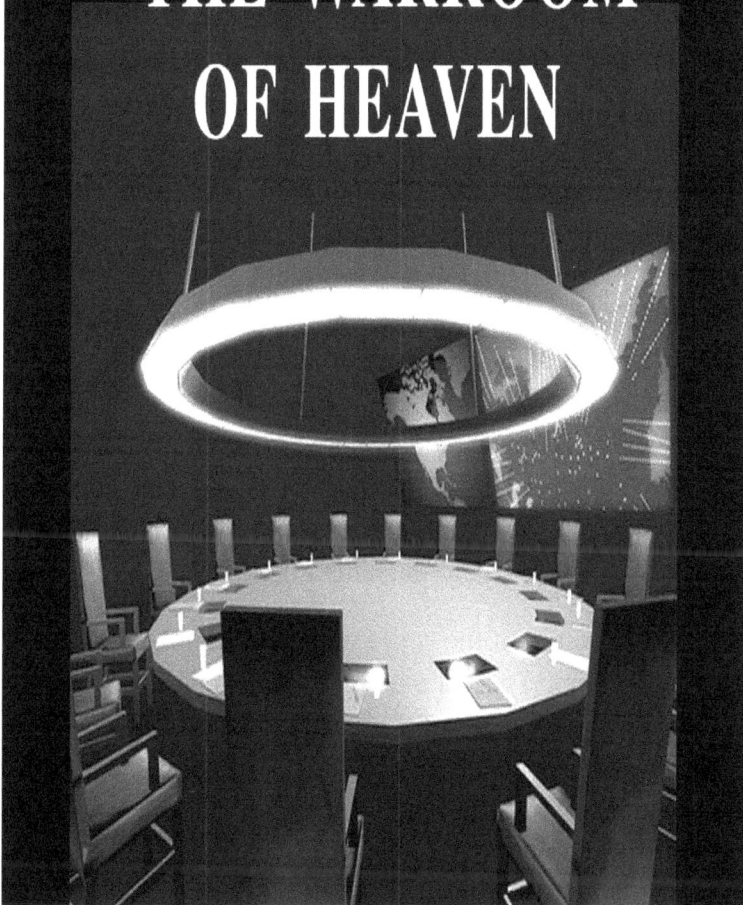

THE WAR ROOM OF HEAVEN

I find myself in great room, along with others, wearing the Golden Armor of God. There are also warrior angels in the chamber. These fearsome looking creatures are different from the worshiping and from the ministering angels that I have seen before. These warrior angels have a firm and resolute look about them. The smallest of these angels are twice as tall and muscular as any man I have ever seen. Their armor is beautiful and durable, glowing with the power and the glory of God. If you see one of these up close, you want to hear them say, "Fear Not." It is then that I realize we are in, for lack of a better description a Heavenly War Room. Angels are coming and going constantly. There is a great angel in the middle. He is larger than the other angels in the room. The sword he is carrying is as long as I am tall (I am 6 feet 1 inch). I assume it is an archangel giving orders to the other angels.

On the walls are maps of the entire universe. Angels were going in out of these maps. These are more than just maps. These are portals or gateways to areas of the spiritual and the physical universe. There was one entire wall, filled with the planet earth. Most of the activity has earth at its center. Angels are always coming from and going to earth.

THE WAR ROOM OF HEAVEN

Then, the Archangel said, "The Lord God has declared, it is time for this stronghold to fall."

Suddenly, the wall of earth melts away, and there is a stronghold of evil. What we are seeing is more than a 3-D picture; it also showed its purpose and the principality over it. It was the stronghold of control and manipulation. It was large covering hundreds of miles and hundreds of miles high.

The stronghold's walls were massive, and its' gate thick. It also had a thick darkness of evil covering it and the surrounding area. It had what looked like tentacles of darkness stretching out hundreds of miles in every direction. We could see the hundreds of demons moving in and out of the stronghold.

The Archangel continued, "This is why you are all here, at this time. The Lord God has ordained that this stronghold is to fall and you are to use His power and authority to win this victory.

You have the most powerful of all the weapons of God within you. This weapon is Worship and Praise. Worship and Praise are the words of your testimony, and the enemy has no weapon to defend against it.

THE WAR ROOM OF HEAVEN

When Worship and Praise come from your hearts, nothing can stop its power, for the Lord God Creator inhabits your praise and worship.

 We, the Army of the Lord of Hosts, will also be with you in this battle, and we will appear at the appointed time."

THE STRONGHOLD

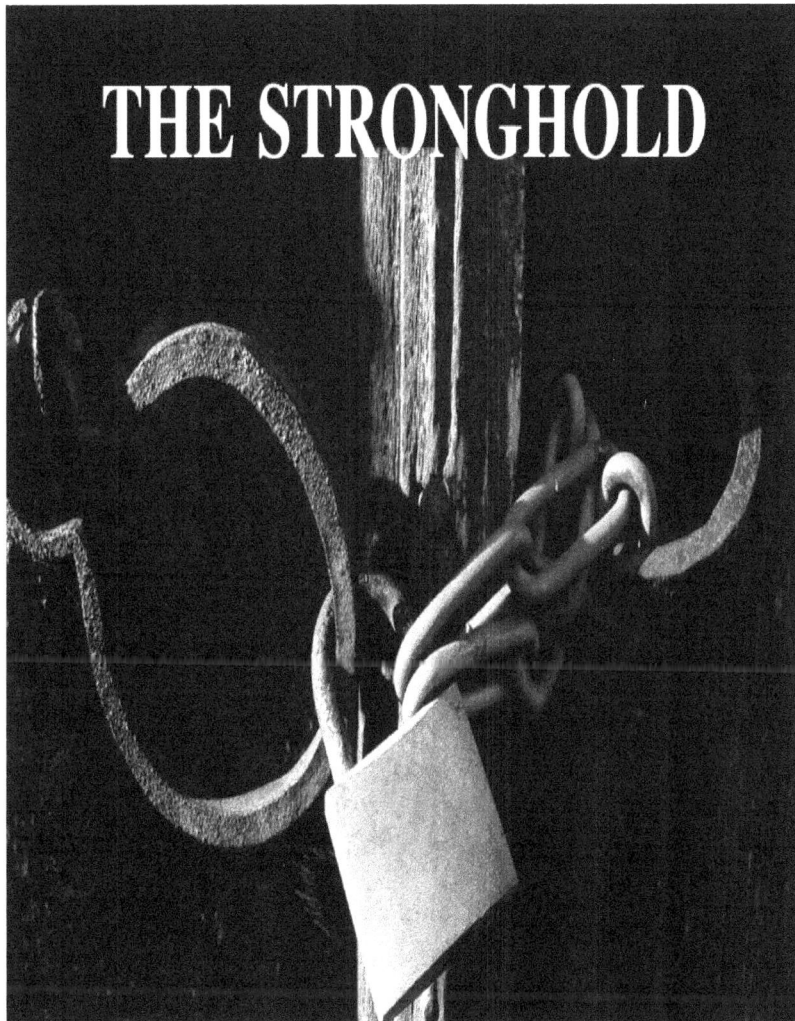

THE STRONGHOLD

Afterward, I found myself back in the camp of the Army of God. Orders begin to flow from my mouth and from the others who were in the war room. Shofars sound, the troops, form up, and we start to march. We soon find ourselves, surrounding this massive stronghold of evil, the fortress of control and manipulation.

In the Heavenly War Room the fortress looked impressive, but standing in front of it, it was massive. The stronghold stretched skyward for what seemed like a hundred miles, and all we could see was its thick dark walls.

There was also a thick cloud of darkness surrounding the stronghold, and you could almost taste the evil in the atmosphere. If it were not for the fact, that God had ordained this stronghold to fall, its appearance could cause even the most faithful to spring back.

We could hear the shouts from the evil forces inside the stronghold. There were tens of thousands of demons inside, and they made a terrible noise. The demons screamed at us, "To give up, to drop your shields for this stronghold will never be destroyed."

THE STRONGHOLD

This screaming at us raises my faith; I remember that their leader, the devil, is a liar and the father of lies and the truth is not in him. The demons also are liars and cannot tell the truth. So, everything they scream at us is a lie. Suddenly, they unleash waves of fiery arrows at us, but our Shields of Faith absorbed every one of them.

In unison, shofars sound, and we worship and praise our Lord and Father. At first, nothing seems to be happening. The demons begin to laugh at us and mock us. Then an amazing thing happens, the walls of the stronghold start to crack, and the gates begin to dissolve.

The scripture came to my mind, "the gates of hell shall not prevail against the church." The demons stopped laughing and start screaming at us again. This time they yelled for us to halt the attack, for we have already won. At the same time, it came to me by the Holy Spirit, "press the attack to destroy this stronghold. This fortress has been attacked many times, but my people have stopped short of total victory. Now is the time for complete victory; do not stop until you win."

THE STRONGHOLD

At this, I worshiped and praised God pressing in even more. The others around me do the same. A great light suddenly breaks out of heaven, striking the stronghold.

The warrior angels poured forth, covering the fortress in light, and the light grows brighter and brighter. Until, out of the center of the stronghold an evil force emerged, screaming and streaking away, faster than any missile I have ever seen. The light (the Glory of God) grew even brighter. I had to close my eyes, as we continued to worship. Finally, the worship and praise settle down. I opened my eyes; the stronghold is no longer there. In its place, is a portal between heaven and earth (what some call an open heaven).

The portal itself stretches skyward, higher than the stronghold that was there. It is also wider. The portal glows with the Glory of God. Its color is golden, and there is a multitude of colors in it and radiating out of it. The Glory of God is flowing out of it onto the earth and angels are ascending and descending.

As I am watching all of this, my mind begins to wonder. What was that force of evil that flew over us?

THE STRONGHOLD

The Holy Spirit answers, "That was the principality of control and manipulation fleeing. Do not worry about him, his day is almost over, and his judgment is coming soon."

We all start worshipping, and we hear the voice of the Lord saying, "I will take back what is mine, I will restore, and I will renew, I will bring My Glory to every corner of the earth once again. No power or principality will be able to stop what I have ordained to do. The hour of victory is now, and restoration for my people and the restoration of My Glory covering the earth, as the waters cover the sea."

We all shouted and wept with joy in the Presence of our Father, the Almighty God. As we finished our worship, I stood looking at the portal. I watched in awe, as the Glory of God flowed out of the portal onto the earth. All different types of angels were coming and going.

I watched this beautiful sight for what seemed like hours. The Glory had many colors, all pulsating with light as if it was a living rainbow of infinite colors.

THROUGH
THE PORTAL

THROUGH THE PORTAL

I felt a stirring, from deep within me, to move closer to the portal. The closer to the entrance the harder it gets. The hardest is due to the force of the River of Glory flowing out of the portal. I had to stop and worship every so often. Waves of Glory wash around and through me. I continue to press towards the portal.

I finally reach the massive gateway. It glows and pulsates with the Power of God and stretching for hundreds of miles in every direction. It has many colors radiating from it. Some of the colors I know from earth, but there are other colors so beautiful and amazing, they are beyond description.

There is a new urging from within my spirit, to step into the Portal. While my human nature screams a 1000 "what ifs"? After a time of great conflict within myself, I praise the Lord as I step into the portal.

Immediately, I find myself back in the War Room of Heaven. The Archangel is standing directly in front of me, and I am unsure of what to do. The Archangel does not say a word but gives me a wink and smile and points to a doorway; I had not seen this door on my previous visit.

THROUGH THE PORTAL

I give a great sigh of relief, and decided that a wink and a smile from an Archangel is much better than just a "fear not."

As I go through the door, there is a refreshing breeze of the Holy Spirit that blows through me. It is wonderful; I did not realize how tired I had become. As this breeze of the Spirit flows, it is as if every cell in my body is receiving refreshing at the same time.

Looking at my surroundings, I find myself in a beautiful garden, which stretches out before me in every direction as far as one could see. I want to explore this beautiful place, walking in the garden. I would stop and smell the flowers. The scent of these flowers has a renewing and healing effect on my spirit, soul, and body. After walking for a while, the garden opens into a pasture. In the middle of this field is a beautiful pond.

The water in the pond is perfectly still, yet as with everything here, it seems to be full of life. Looking back the way I came, I was surprised to see no evidence of me walking in the garden or the pasture. Everything was perfect. I decided to do an experiment.

THROUGH THE PORTAL

I pressed my foot down hard on the ground and lifted it up, and the grass immediately sprang back into place. You could almost hear the joy rising from the grass as this happened. Then I tried the same thing with the sand around the pond, and it happens again.

I walked along the edge of this pond for a while. Then I sat down to rest, and then I lie down. As I drifted off to sleep, I remembered Psalm 23; the Lord is my shepherd I shall not want. He makes me lie down in green pastures, He leads me beside still waters, and He restores my soul

I woke up surrounded by the Glory so bright; it is like looking into a noonday sun. I shielded my eyes, so that could see. There amid the Glory is Jesus. He reaches out His hand to me and helps me to my feet. We walk, a great distance in silence. I am enjoying Jesus' company, and I sense that He was enjoying mine.

We stop, and Jesus turned to me and said, "Keep doing what you are doing.

THROUGH THE PORTAL

Keep warring against demons, principalities, and powers, for I HAVE ALREADY GIVEN YOU THE VICTORY.

I also want you to tell my people who they are in me and where they are now, My authority and My power are available to them and them."

At this, I fell to my knees and said, "But Lord I don't understand who I am and who your people are in you. How can I tell them what I don't know?"

Jesus lifts me up and says, "I will teach you and show you who my people are. Most of my people don't know who they are in me. If you do not tell them, many of them will go into unnecessary hardships and attacks from the evil one and his forces. Many will fall away."

With these words, tears began to flow down His cheeks and down mine.

Jesus speaks again, "You must pray that their eyes will be open and that ears will be open to hear what I am teaching them. They are much more than what they think.

THROUGH THE PORTAL

They are not just worshippers, warriors or believers; <u>THEY ARE MUCH, MUCH MORE AS ARE YOU.</u> Will you teach them, as I teach you?

 I say, "Yes, Lord I will."

Jesus said, "There will be many who will misunderstand and even say evil about you, as they did with me. Are you still willing?

 I say, "Yes Lord."

 Jesus spoke again, "Then as I showed you my heart many years ago and My Heart is transforming your heart, so this will be for you. I will show you these things and will teach you, and you will teach my people. You will write and teach them. For now, continue the battles, continue the war."

 Then Jesus placed His hands on my chest. I felt the Glory of God flow through me and around me. I closed my eyes and worshiped. When I opened my eyes, I am back on the other side of the portal.

THE GATEKEEPERS

THE GATEKEEPERS

I found myself caught up in the Spirit once again. This time I am walking through an arid land. There are trees, but they have no leaves, and the ground is rock hard and cracked. Even the breeze is hot, dry and dusty. I use the Shield of Faith to protect my face from the dust as I move forward. I walk for many miles in this dry, dusty land, until I come to a dry riverbed. The riverbed is wider than the Mississippi River. I noticed in the middle of the riverbed a small stream, so small you can easily cross it in one step, but the water in it flowed clean and pure.

Around the edges of the stream, there are small patches of grass, the first signs of life I have seen in this dry land. I feel an urge to go upstream; at least I would have fresh water to drink.

As I walk, the breeze continues to blow. At times it was as if the breeze was groaning. The land itself was crying for relief from the dryness that was all around me. After traveling many miles upstream, I saw something appear in the distance. As I came closer, it grew larger. At first, I thought it was a rain cloud, and I made a quick note of how far away the edge of the riverbed was, just in case I needed to move quickly from the river. I soon realize that it was a high mountain rising before me.

THE GATEKEEPERS

As I reached the mountain, I took note that the mountain is as dry as the land around it. Nearby there was a massive dam, and it is as big as the mountain itself, stretching from one side to the other and reaching skyward. The dam and the mountain were so high that I could not see the top. I also noticed that the small stream was coming down the side of the dam.

It was late in the day. So, I decided to make camp for the night and get a fresh start up the mountain in the morning. I knew that I needed to climb to the top of the mountain, but it would be safer to climb during the day.

I awoke the next morning and took a drink from the stream. Immediately I am refreshed and strengthened. With a full canteen, I prepare to climb. I sling the Shield of Faith onto my back and with my knife cut out hand holds and footholds. The ground of the mountain was just as dry as the rest of the land, making it difficult to dig out handholds and footholds. It was very hard to climb.

As I climbed the mountain, I passed seven massive floodgates. Each gate is twelve stories high. The gates were shut tight with only a little stream coming out of one them.

THE GATEKEEPERS

I thought to myself, who would keep these gates closed? The land below needed the water and needed it so badly. I continued my climb to the top of the mountain.

Closer to the top of the mountain, the ground became moist, making it easier to climb. Closer to the top, a refreshing spray of water came off the mountain and made me feel renewed and refreshed. I finally reached the top of the mountain and the dam. I turned around and saw a huge reservoir. The reservoir stretches as far as I can see. Around the reservoir, the land is beautiful and green. There were many kinds of fruit trees as well as oak and pine trees. There was life everywhere. I sense the Presence of God everywhere around me.

The reservoir is so full, that some of the water laps over the top of the dam. I noticed that there were seven large hand cranks on top of the dam. These cranks opened the floodgates. Feeling the urging of the Spirit to turn the hand cranks, I turned the first crank, and it turned easily (to my surprise), and the first gate opened.

THE GATEKEEPERS

There was a shudder in the dam, looking over the edge, I see the water pouring down to the river bed far below from one of the floodgates.

I quickly returned and opened all the floodgates. I went back to the edge of the dam and saw that there was great and powerful waterfall flowing down the side. As I look out at the land far below, the river now flows in its fullness through the land. From the riverbanks, it spreads outward making land beautiful and green. The transformation was amazing; the dry and dusty land had become a lush, green beautiful paradise.

I turned around to check the reservoir, and to my surprise, it was overflowing. Even with thousands of gallons of water flowing out of the floodgates, water was running everywhere, even down the side of the mountain.

Then, I felt the master's hand on my shoulder, so I turned and looked into His wonderful face and glorious eyes and immediately began to worship Him.

THE GATEKEEPERS

Jesus spoke, "Well done my son, you opened the floodgates and watering the earth by My Spirit. You see, the earth was dry and groaning, as you heard. The earth is groaning for the revealing of the Sons of God. The dam and the mountain are the heart of each person. Every one of my children has a reservoir and floodgates. It is up to each, to open the gates and to let all that I Am flow out of them to the earth.

In this matter, the Sons of God are being revealed to the earth, and the refreshing of the earth occurs when the floodgates of their hearts are open. Many of them hold the gates closed or only open the gates a little. They do this out of fear that there is not enough of the water of the Spirit and they will run out. They do not realize that I am more than sufficient and the more they allow My Spirit to flow out to the earth, the more I will pour in much more than they are allowing to flow and I will overflow them."

Then I said to the Lord, "The floodgates I just opened are my gates to open and close. They are a part of my heart."

The Lord says, "Yes you are correct.

THE GATEKEEPERS

These are yours, and this is your heart. You must decide every day to open the gates or keep them closed."

The Lord continues, "Each one of my children is a Gatekeeper of the Reservoir of the Spirit within their hearts. My desire is for you and them to keep the gates open.

The seven floodgates represent the 7-Fold Spirit of God within you. Out of each gate flows the Fruits of the Spirit and the Gifts of the Spirit. Each gate has a fruit and a gift. The additional two Fruits of the Spirit and the two additional Gifts of the Spirits flow out of all the gates. The two Fruits of the Spirit that flow out of all the gates are love and peace without these the gifts cannot efficiently operate.

The two Fruits of the Spirit that flow out of all the gates are faith and wisdom, for without faith the gifts cannot function, and without wisdom, the gifts can be misused and abused. Again, I say you were right this is your heart.

The mountain you climbed, the dam, the floodgates, and the reservoir are all parts of your heart."

THE GATEKEEPERS

"Lord," I say, "When I started to climb, the bottom part of my heart was dry as the earth."

Jesus said, "That is right, and as you climbed closer to the top, to the reservoir, the ground became moist and beautiful and easier to climb."

I said, "Yes, Lord."

Then the Lord speaks, "The reason is this. The reservoir was only overflowing a little, and only the top levels of the heart were benefiting from the refreshing water of the Spirit. Now, that you have opened the floodgates, I will pour out a greater overflow that will flow down to the lowest parts of your heart. The movement of the River of Fruits and the Gifts of the Spirit is to benefit the earth. The overflow from the reservoir is to benefit you. The overflow is true for all my children, the more you open the floodgates, and the more I will flood and soak your heart in My Spirit. My heart for you and all my children that you will be Gatekeepers that keep the floodgates open.

THE GATEKEEPERS

I fell to the ground in worship, and when I looked up, I was back in my chair hearing, "Be the gatekeeper that keeps the floodgate open."

THE LAND OF THE

CLOSED GATES

THE LAND OF THE CLOSED GATES

I find myself walking with Jesus through the land that was once dry and is now beautiful since the River of the Spirit began to flow after the floodgates were open. The earth and all it holds seem to be rejoicing.

We stopped along the river, and Jesus said, "Fill your canteen from the river. Here are six more canteens, fill them also. You are going on a journey, and you will need them."

After filling all the canteens, we continued to walk. I wondered what type of journey I was going on. I knew Jesus would tell me in the fullness of time. As we walk along, I begin picking different kinds of fruit and place them in my supply sack. We finally come to a place where the land begins dry and dusty.

Jesus turns to me and says, "You must cross this land to reach the Mountains of Refreshing on the other side."

I looked up and saw on the horizon the very tips of the mountains. The Master continued, "This is the Land of the Closed Gates."

"Why is it called the Land of the Closed Gates? "I ask.

THE LAND OF THE CLOSED GATES

Jesus replies, "It is a land where the people have closed the gates of the hearts and they, like the land, have become dry. They live in deception and eat and drink the fruit of deception. These are still my people, they walked with me once, but now they are trapped by deception."

I noticed that tears were in Jesus' eyes as He spoke. Then He said, "It is good that you picked fruit and you have water from the River of the Spirit. You must not eat or drink anything that is on the land unless it overtakes you."

I say, "There is nothing in that land that I want."

The Lord put His hands on my shoulders, turned me entirely towards him and said in a firm voice, "There is water there, and there is fruit. There are seven pools of water, each surrounded by an oasis. The seven pools of water are seven deceptions and the fruits, are the fruits of deception. Do Not eat or drink of deception."

I bowed down and worshiped Jesus and when I looked up He was gone.

THE LAND OF THE CLOSED GATES

Having walked many hours in the dry Land of the Closed Gates, I climb a ridge and see an oasis in the valley below. From a distance, the oasis is beautiful to the eyes. As I come down the ridge, I notice that there is a paved road leading to the oasis.

I remember the warning of Jesus, not to eat the fruit or drink the water in this land. I took out some of the fruit I picked and ate it and drank the water from one of the canteens. Upon entering the oasis, the people I passed looked at me with concern, but they say nothing and turn back to what they were doing.

The buildings that looked so beautiful from a distance don't look nearly as good up close. The buildings need minor repairs and maintenance. Some need painting and others need a window or a door fixed. The people have the tools and the paint, but they just stand there looking at what needs to be done then shrug and walk away. There seems to be a lot of indifference here.

The center of the oasis, there is the pool that feeds the oasis. Some weeds have grown up all around it. There are fruit trees, but they are unattended.

THE LAND OF THE CLOSED GATES

The trees have fruit that is ripe and ready to be picked. A lot of the fruit has fallen from the trees and has rotted on the ground. There are men and women there, but they don't to seem care. They only pick what they need from the trees and draw enough water from the fountain for their needs.

I try and warn them about the fruit and the water and its effect on them. I talk to the people about winning the lost and opening the floodgates of their hearts and let the River of the Spirit flow.

They listen, and some say, "Just relax, whatever happens, will happen.

Some would say, "When Jesus wants to do something he'll do it. It's all up to him."

Still, others would say," That nice." and they walk away. They didn't care that I was talking about having an active relationship with God and reaching out to those who do not know God. They didn't care that I was doing those things and they didn't care that they were not doing those things.

Truly, this is a place of indifference. I am amazed by the indifference and the lack of caring of these people.

THE LAND OF THE CLOSED GATES

The night is beginning to fall, and I decide I would rather sleep on the dry ground than spend a night in this place. I quickly headed out of the oasis and to my surprise, no one tried to stop me from leaving. I should not be surprised, due to the indifference that is there.

I reached the top of the ridge on the other side of the oasis, and the paved road comes to an end. Back on the dirt path, I start down the side of the ridge. Moving down the ridge, I notice a cave off to the side of the road. The cave is not very high, and I have to bend over to enter.

The cave is only about 5-foot-high and maybe 10-foot-wide and about 10 foot deep. It is the perfect place to stop and rest. I built a fire at the entrance and settled in for the night. I thought over the day's events. The walk and talk with Jesus and his warning to me. I reflect on the oasis of indifference and the people I met there. They did not even realize what indifference had done to them and how trapped they were.

I begin to pray that God will break through the deception in their lives. After praying I dosed off to sleep.

THE LAND OF THE CLOSED GATES

The sun shining into the cave wakes me. I prepared for the days walk. I ate some more fruit and drank some refreshing water. I feel the resurgence of God's Spirit in my spirit and a renewed strength flowing into my body.

Stepping out of the cave, I felt a strong wind against my body and the dust pelting my face. Quickly, I retreat into the cave. I pulled out a robe from my supply sack. I remembered the Master giving it to me as we neared the Land of the Closed Gates.

Jesus said, "You will need this robe from time to time. Keep it with you at all times." I took the robe and thanked Jesus for it and put it carefully in my supply sack.

The robe was plain looking on the outside, but the lining was beautiful. It has a tapestry of red, royal blue, silver, and gold threads. It's woven into a beautiful and powerful roaring lion with fire coming out of the mouth. It fits perfectly. It has a belt to close the robe when, and a hood and even an attached scarf to wrap around my face. I got a mental picture of myself and laughed out loud. I looked like a medieval monk or someone out of a Lawrence of Arabia movie.

THE LAND OF THE CLOSED GATES

The wind is still blowing strong as I leave the cave. I walk at a brisk pace with the sure-footedness of the Holy Spirit leading me.

After traveling most of the day, I come to the top of a small ridge and see the oasis off in the distance. It is too far for me to reach before nightfall so I would be spending the night on the road. After several more hours on the road (path), and fighting against the relentless wind, I came to the bridge that crosses a gorge.

I checked out the underside of the bridge and found that it is a perfect place to spend the night. It is out of the wind and has wood lying around to build a fire. I shake my robe, and a lot of dust and dirt fall off. I am very grateful to have the robe. I hate to think what that dust and dirt would have done to me without the robe to protect me. With this thought, I praised the Lord for His protection. After I had eaten and drank, I pulled my robe over me and fell fast asleep.

In the morning, my body is telling me that sleeping on the ground is a young man's game, and I am not as young as I used to be. The wind is still blowing. I quickly eat and drink, restoring my strength.

THE LAND OF THE CLOSED GATES

It amazes me how quickly the water from the River of God and its fruit energize me. I put my robe on and headed out.

I drew near this oasis, and immediately notice this place is different. Even from a distance, I can see that this place needs a lot of work. The paved road has potholes and ruts. The buildings could use painting and some repairs. Some even have broken windows. It looks like it has been that way for a long time.

The people of the oasis are curious about me. They say, "We don't get many travelers wearing robes passing through."

I state, "I am traveling to a beautiful distant land."

They respond, "It sounds great. Maybe someday we will do the same. "It was the same when we talked about doing the good works of God that He had prepared for them to do.

They made the same statement, "Maybe someday."

Again, and again, I would talk about doing, and they would say, "I need to sleep on it" or "I need to pray about it" or others would say, "Sounds great, but I will start to tomorrow."

THE LAND OF THE CLOSED GATES

Truly, this is the Oasis of Procrastination. I am determined not to spend one night in this place. The evening was fast approaching as I passed the Pool of Procrastination, so I quickened my pace out of the oasis. Night had fallen as I looked back towards the oasis. I noticed that there seemed to be procrastination even about turning on the lights.

Moving well into the night, I was being urged forward by the Spirit of God. I finally come to a place, where there were some trees. There were leaves piled on the ground. I could move off the trail and be unseen by any passerby, and the leaves would make a great bed. I thanked the Lord, for not having to sleep on the hard ground.

The next morning, I continue my journey. After a few hours of travel, I heard sounds; soon I can understand clearly, it is the sound of music. I round the bend in the road there is the oasis. Unlike the other oasis, this place is beautiful with lots of buildings gleaming in the sun. As I enter the oasis, the buildings are impressive, and the streets were beautiful and clean. The sound of music was everywhere, but something was not right.

THE LAND OF THE CLOSED GATES

Every person I met is well dressed and talks about the blessings of the Lord and how much money they made. The closer I move to the pool in the center of the oasis, the fewer people talked about the Lord and the more they talked about wealth.

There were some who questioned why I was wearing such an everyday robe. I explained that I was traveling and the robe suited that purpose. The inhabitants said that I was wise, for they heard rumors that there were robbers on the road.

There were some who wanted to see what I was wearing under the robe. When, the people had caught a glimpse of it, and it looked beautiful. I untied the robe and let it fall open, revealing the Armor of God.

They immediately began shouting at me, "You're radical, you have come to stir up trouble," "Why don't you believe in the blessings of God," "Why, are you here? Get out, " and still others yelled, "You have come to disrupt the peace."

I quickly sling the Shield of Faith in front of me, for these beautiful people, suddenly became not so nice. They began throwing things at me, including the fruit they were eating.

THE LAND OF THE CLOSED GATES

I pulled out the Sword of the Spirit, and then I realized that
these are people of God. They are in deception, but they are His.
They all are under the deception of earthly wealth and talk of
prosperity.

I quickly outdistanced the angry mob, which was easy because
they were all eating and drinking and were made fat by the
deception. I make my way out of the oasis. Once, I was a safe
distance away; I stopped to rest.

It was then that I noticed, the fruit that they had thrown at me
hit the Shield of Faith and my robe had become rotten and was
dry. All it took was a brush of my hand the rotten fruit fell off
the shield; I shook the robe with the same effect.

What surprised me was when the fruit hit the ground, it
immediately turned to dust. I poured a little of the water from
the River of God on my hands and the Shield of Faith to clean
them. As I clean the Shield, it begins to glow with the Power of
God. I climbed a high ridge and as night fell and I looked down
to see the lights of the oasis's I had previously visited.

THE LAND OF THE CLOSED GATES

As I stand atop the ridge, I raise the glowing Shield of Faith and the Sword of the Spirit. The sword, the Armor of God and robe are glowing with the power of God. The power flows up into the night sky; it is as if I have become a beacon of the Spirit. The light sweeps across the land, like a searchlight. It settles on each oasis, and the ground under my feet is shaking with the power of God. The flow of power fades, and I let down my arms.

The Shield continues to glow, as I take the time to eat and drink. Afterward, I start down the other side of the ridge.

As I move down the other side of the ridge, the Shield of Faith is still glowing. I come upon a cave with light coming from the inside. I enter the cave, and there stood an angel.

The angel said, "Welcome mighty warrior, highly favored of God. Come in and rest and eat."

It is a large cave with a pool of water, Fed by a stream coming out of the wall. The food was cooking on the fire.

THE LAND OF THE CLOSED GATES

. The angel speaks again, "Please, take your rest. I have been sent to refresh and reward you for the good you have done. Remove your robe and relax. Enjoy what I have prepared for you, a mighty man of God."

The offer sounds splendid to me after what I had just been through I am tired, and rest and refreshing, just what I need. As I sit down, I take a quick glance into the Shield of Faith. The reflection of the angel appears, but it is no angel. It is a demon, its true nature revealed by faith.

In one swift move, I draw the Sword of the Spirit and pin the beast to the wall with the tip of the sword at its throat.

"I command you to reveal who are." Immediately, the light fades away and before me, stands a creature of darkness. I can see the hate in his eyes and the absolute contempt for me on his face. He dares not move, for the sword still, has him pinned and I now have the Shield of Faith between us.

I ask again, "Who are you? What is your name?"

THE LAND OF THE CLOSED GATES

The demon begins to speak, "I am…" I quickly can tell he is going to try to lie.

I press the sword a little harder against his throat and say, "The truth."

The demon says, "I am one of the spirits of false acceptance, and this is my oasis."

Then I say, "You were sent here to deceive me and keep me in this cave."

It answered, "Yes."

I say, "This is going to cost you. I command you to go where Jesus would send you."

With that power, the demon vanishes. I kick over the food.

Then I reach for one of my canteens and pour the water from the River of the Spirit of God into the pool of false acceptance. The ground begins to quake, the rocks in the ceiling begin to fall. I quickly, run out of the cave. The cave collapses into a pile of rubble and dust.

THE LAND OF THE CLOSED GATES

The dawn has come. I did not realize, that I had been in the cave all night or I that I may have been there even longer. This thought sends a chill down my spine. The deception of false acceptance is powerful.

As the sun rises, I see that a significant portion of the mountain, all the way up to the ridge, has collapsed. I move clear of the dust and rubble and take the time to refresh myself with water from the river and the fruit from my bag. I climb down the mountain and get back on the trail and quickly move away from the mountain.

I stop to catch my breath when I hear a rumble and then an explosion. Looking back and see the whole mountain is on fire and lava was pouring down its sides.

It is then that I realize by faith and the water of the Spirit of God destroys the place of deception. It will be a very long time before this location could be used for deception again.

THE LAND OF THE CLOSED GATES

Walking away, I meditated on all the recent events of this journey. The oasis of indifference, procrastination, wealth and false acceptance, were deceptions that I had in my life. I drop to my knees, crying out in repentance. I ask Jesus to forgive me and to wash me and restore righteousness to me.

As I was praying, a cloud appeared in the clear sky and rain began to fall. It was as refreshing as a spring rain washing the dirt and grime from where I had been.

I immediately begin to praise the Lord for His love, forgiveness, and refreshing. Even the earth around me benefited from the shower. All around me there were beautiful flowers. I knew I could not stay here long. I ate and drank and with a new determination, set out for my next destination.

I am coming into the next oasis. This one is different than the others. There are well-kept buildings and the streets. It is a simple place, almost like those small towns in 1950's American television. It looks too good to be true. The people are very friendly and are willing to talk with you.

THE LAND OF THE CLOSED GATES

I spoke with a middle-aged man about Jesus.

He quickly cut me off and said, "We don't talk about Jesus."

I asked him, "Why not?"

He said, "We don't want to offend anyone."

Again, and again, every time I mentioned Jesus or the Power of the Holy Spirit. They would say, please don't talk about that, because it might cause trouble and they didn't want any trouble or to offend anyone.

Still, others would say, "Religion is a personal matter not discussed in public."

Some people would state, "That they go to church and it is there and only there where we can talk about religion." And there were those who firmly asked me, to leave their town before I caused trouble.

Truly an Oasis of Denial. Everyone there Knew about God but, denied Him and His power, so as not to offend anyone.

THE LAND OF THE CLOSED GATES

I left this oasis with great sadness in my heart for the people living under this deception. I continued down the trail and as was my custom I ate and drank as I went.

It was only a few hours before I entered the next oasis. There are lots of people moving about, and there is much work that needs competition.

Some of the buildings were half finished, and others are needing repair. There were weeds everywhere, and the fruit trees were in a word, a mess.

I talked with many of the people, they all knew what the needs are but, all said, "Someone else would do it." There was a complete lack of responsibility. No one would even take the responsibility to pick up a piece of paper because someone else would do it. And if you did do something, it proved their point. In spiritual matters, this is true as well. Their philosophy was, someone else will witness, someone will pray, and someone else will study the Word of God. It was nearly impossible, to make any headway with these people. The more I tried, the more I proved their way of thinking.

THE LAND OF THE CLOSED GATES

It was incredibly frustrating. I was glad to leave this Oasis of Irresponsibility behind, but I was sorrowful for the people.

Leaving the oasis, I noticed a strange darkness on the horizon. Further down the road, the darkness grew larger.

I stopped and ate and drank from my provisions, sensing that all my strength would be needed. I move into the darkness it took hours to reach the oasis.

I entered the oasis; the darkness became greater and heavier on me. I was having trouble making out the buildings in the dark. Most of the people moved away from me as I approached them. The fear in this place is so intense you can almost taste it. The few people I could talk with were hopelessly in fear. They had a fear of rejection, fear of destruction, fear of the devil, fear of failure and even the fear of success. The Oasis is the largest of the oases.

The closer I get to the center of the oasis, the more fear presses down on me. I drink more of the water and eat more of the fruit I have with me, and I gain strength.

THE LAND OF THE CLOSED GATES

The darkness of fear is pressing in from all sides, it so close that I can only see a foot or less in front of me. I continue to push forward. My strength was fading fast. Then I hear a voice saying, "You are not going to make it." I heard that the same voice in 2007, saying the same thing when I was about to have quadruple by-pass surgery.

It was wrong then, and I determined that voice would be wrong now. The fear continued to close in on all sides and voices of defeat were growing louder and louder.

Then, I heard a voice from deep within my spirit, "Turn the Robe inside out." I immediately stopped and turned the robe inside out. The Lion on the robe started to glow; I felt the fire and the power of the Holy Spirit rising in me, I did not realize how weak I had become. Then, I brought the Shield of Faith in front of me, and it also begins to glow. The Sword of the Spirit lighted up like a torch.

THE LAND OF THE CLOSED GATES

With all the light around me, I now see the gate leading out of the oasis, just a few short feet in front of me. I quickly move through the gate and then down the road, until I am well clear of the darkness. I knelt and praised the Lord for getting me out of the Oasis of fear.

Then, I prayed for those trapped there and in every oasis of deception and fear. After prayer, I notice it is still daylight, which is surprising to me. It felt like I had been in the Oasis of Fear a long time.

THE MOUNTAINS
OF REFRESHING

THE MOUNTAINS OF REFRESHING

The mountains are close as the trail moved into them. The mountain walls now tower above me on each side of the path. Suddenly, the trail ends and before me is a thick forest. I knew that I could not go back, so I pressed forward into the woods. I pull out the Sword of the Spirit, to cut a path through the trees, but the trees separate. I put the sword away, and the trees close together. Then I pulled out the sword again and moved forward, and the trees are moving apart in front of me. I look behind me the trees have closed. I continued and noticed that the colors of the leaves on the trees and even the color of the trees are getting brighter and becoming more alive. There is the sound of a mighty waterfall. I've heard the noise of this water before.

It is the sound of joy that the water of the River of God makes as it flows from the Throne of God. As I step into a clearing, there it is the waterfall. It is beautiful and stretches skyward until it disappears in the clouds. Just looking at it is refreshing to my soul.

There is a lagoon created by the waterfall. The water is crystal clear. I move to the other end of the pool I see another waterfall with the River of God flowing down to the earth.

THE MOUNTAINS OF REFRESHING

It is then that I realize how high up I am in the mountains. The view is so beautiful and amazing. Puffs of clouds are below me, and eagles are soaring through the sky. I could stand here for hours enjoying this view, and in fact, I have. Turning back and walk away from the edge, I see life everywhere.

This place is the total opposite of the Oasis of Fear. It is wonderful and beautiful! Even the air I breathe here seems to be alive with joy and peace.

Wading into the lagoon; my body glows with life and joy. Overwhelmed with joy, I dive into the water and begin to swim and to shout and to play like a little kid. I climbed on a rock and watched this beautiful and refreshing scene.

I decide to move over to the waterfall, where the spray is wonderful. I step into the waterfall; an amazing thing happened, I rose. The water below is forcing me upward and the water above parts as I rise. The water around me continues downward with tremendous force.

THE MOUNTAINS OF REFRESHING

As I look, I see the entire Land of Closed Gates before me. Over to my right, I can see the River of the Spirit and the beauty of the surrounding area. Soon I am passing through the clouds and reach the top of the mountain. I step over onto the land; I look up, and there stands Jesus smiling.

Jesus says, "Welcome to the Mountains of Refreshing."

I fell, at his feet in worship. I cried, "I failed! I barely made it out of the Land of Closed Gates and then only with your help. I didn't bring anyone with me."

Jesus raised his hand and said, "You did not fail, Come with me."

We walked away from the edge of the mountain. The beauty of this place is overwhelming. There are flowers and trees everywhere, yet there is a perfect order in this place adding to its beauty. We stopped; I turned and looked down into a valley far, below. The Land of Closed Gates stretches out before me. I see hundreds of people moving out of the different oasis. I turn back to Jesus with tears in my eyes.

THE MOUNTAINS OF REFRESHING

Jesus says, "You did not fail. Those people, who are moving down there, are moving due to the example you were to them. You showed them that there is something better than they had. They once again have hope, and their faith has begun to grow within them again."

I am stunned, at what I am seeing and hearing. I fall at Jesus' feet and again worship him.

Jesus lifts me up, and we walked beside the river, which flows clean and clear. The trees are all fruit bearing, and amazing. The air itself is alive with the Spirit of God. As we round the bend, the land unfolds before me. The view is fantastic and exciting. Off in the distance are high mountains that rise into the Glory Cloud of the Father's presence and disappear. The mountains have various buildings; some look like beautiful homes, others look like administrative buildings and still others look like storehouses of some type. These buildings are beautiful, having the glow of the Glory of God. Even from this distance, they are massive.

THE MOUNTAINS OF REFRESHING

From time to time, the Glory Cloud of God's presence would roll down the mountain like a tidal wave, covering everything in its presence. Then, it would roll back up the mountain. When the glory moved back up the mountain, everything on it glowed brighter than a summer sun at noon; I shielded my eyes from the brightness.

To my amazement there are thousands of people, going and coming (as I witnessed before in the Throne Room of God, coming and going, is appearing and disappearing). At seeing this, it came to mind that this was to be a place of refreshing.

Jesus begins to speak, "This is a place of refreshing. On earth, man thinks that refreshing and rest is doing nothing for extended periods of time. They are less rested and refreshed at these times. Have you not experienced this?"

"Yes," I answered.

Jesus continues, "Here refreshing comes from doing the Will of God. You had experienced this when you ministered to my people. After hours of ministry, have you not felt more energized and refreshed than when you started."

THE MOUNTAINS OF REFRESHING

I nodded in agreement.

The Lord continued, "This happens as the Spirit of God flows through you and out to my people. The Spirit of God is life itself, and when the Spirit flows through you, the Spirit deposits life in you. This deposit of life is something that my people must learn. When you minister out of your strength and spirit, it is life draining and wears you out.

But, when you allow the Spirit of God to minister out of you, the Spirit will refresh and give life to you as well as those to which you minister. Remember, I am the vine, you are the branches, when you connect to me there is life.

You may explore as much of the mountains and the valleys of refreshing as you like. Enjoy what I have prepared for you."

With that Jesus was gone. I stand there in awe and wonder for the longest time, and then move forward into the Valley of Refreshing between the Mountains of Refreshing.

THE MOUNTAINS OF REFRESHING

As I come down the side of the mountain, I realize that the valley is far larger than I believed. It seems to stretch for hundreds of miles in every direction. It is beautiful, with streams flowing throughout and fruit trees everywhere.

Walking down the path, I come across one of the streams; dip my hand into the water, and take a drink. The water is refreshing, but the Power of God nearly knocks me down. I hear laughter from behind me. There stands my friend, Gene laughing and saying, "You should know better than to drink from a stream in these high places unprepared. These streams flow from the fountains of the Father and the water in them is directly from the throne of the Father and power in the water is the pure power of God."

We both laugh and embrace and head down the path together, talking about the things of God and wonders we have seen. Then, we come to a fork in the path. I feel the Spirit urging me down one of the paths, but Gene feels the urging to go down the other. We agree to go our separate ways and to meet at the roundtable on earth.

THE MOUNTAINS OF REFRESHING

I come around a bend, and there is a large fountain. The fountain is as tall as the Empire State Building, and the circumference is equal to its height. All around its edge are fruit trees, all bearing the same type of fruit. There are also thousands and thousands of people around the fountain and thousands more coming and going.

Someone from behind me says, "It is the Fountain of Healing."

I turn around, and I am surprised at who is talking to me.

"I am Brother Reinhard," the man says.

"I know, you are the…" he stops me in mid-sentence,

"Those things are not important here. What is important is your relationship with the Father. Learn all you can, spend as much time with him as you can.

As I said, this is the Fountain of Healing, many people come here and receive healing from the Lord, but they don't go beyond this fountain. I come here often, but there is so much more. There are other valleys each with a fountain. There are the Mountains of God, where the manifest Presence of God flows and where you meet with the Father.

81

THE MOUNTAINS OF REFRESHING

I urge you to explore all that God is and develop a deeper relationship with Him. It is in a relationship with Him that you can understand who you truly are and what He is calling you to do."

I say, "I know, I have learned so much already."

Reinhard says, "This is true, but there is so much more. Don't get satisfied where you are. Go beyond where you are God wants you to know Him more. He also has more for you than you imagine. I must go now; I have work to do."

I thanked him for the words of encouragement, and I asked, "Will I see you again?"

Brother Reinhard says, "Perhaps" then gave me a wave of his hand as he walked away and vanished.

I walk around the Fountain of Healing, and there is a path, which I start down. I notice, immediately that this is not near as wide as the one leading to the Fountain of Healing. The trail goes up some hills and crosses several streams.

THE MOUNTAINS OF REFRESHING

The fruit trees begin to change from those that surrounded the Fountain of Healing to another type of tree. These new trees are even more beautiful, and their fruit is larger and tastes amazing.

Entering a clearing, I come to a complete stop in awe of what I see. There before me is a beautiful fountain, at least twice the size of the Fountain of Healing and the water in it seems to glow with the power of God. Also, there are far fewer people around this fountain, than were around the Fountain of Healing. As I approach the fountain, I hear a sound like singing. Closer to the fountain, the sound gets louder. At first, I think it is coming from the fruit trees surrounding the fountain, but it is not coming from them.

The fruit trees themselves are larger than the ones surrounding the Healing Fountain; they are almost as large as oak trees. The fruit on them is the size of round watermelons and have a gold and silver color to them with red stripes mixed inside. I am hungry, so I pick one of these watermelon size pieces of fruit.

THE MOUNTAINS OF REFRESHING

Immediately, as I picked the fruit, a beautiful bloom having the same markings as the fruit, appears. The flower contains in the center of the bloom a tiny miniature of the fruit I just picked.

I sit down and open the watermelon, which to my surprise it opens quickly and is full of seeds. As I eat the meat of the fruit, I begin to feel the love and compassion of God flow all through my spirit, soul, and body. This love and compassion overwhelm me. I think of all the hurting people in the world that need the love of God.

I weep and pray for them, this is a similar in experience as when I was praying, many years ago, asking God to show me His heart. He did it while I was driving a trolley along the oceanfront during one of the many summer festivals we have here in Virginia Beach, Va. It was a life-changing experience for me. I prayed Lord, please lift the experience from me because I couldn't take it anymore and the Father did lift it.

God spoke to me and said, "I had not even scratched the surface of His heart and His love and compassion for all His children."

THE MOUNTAINS OF REFRESHING

I was changed forever by that experience and now what I am feeling is a thousand times more powerful that.

   After what seemed like hours, the power of love and compassion subsidies, but I could still feel it flowing powerfully inside me. I rose and moved toward the fountain. The sound I heard was coming from the water in the fountain. It seemed as if the water was inviting me to drink. I was thirsty, but after the experience with the water of healing, I carefully took a little sip. Instantly, a surge of Holy Power raced through my body, and I am, overcome again.

   I opened my eyes, and once again I am looking up at the sky. I raise up I notice a man sitting on the edge of the fountain. He sees me and comes over and helps me up.

   He introduces himself, "I am John, and no I am not the beloved, for he sits as one of the elders around the throne of God."

   I ask John, "What foundation is this?"

 He replies, "It is the Foundation of Signs and Wonders

of course."

THE MOUNTAINS OF REFRESHING

Then I say, "I would think there would be much more people here at the fountain, for there are many that I know who want to see signs and wonders in their lives."

John responds, "Yes, that is true, but they are not willing to pay the price. They must be prepared to have an intimate relationship with the Holy One and then must be willing to eat of the Fruit of Love and Compassion of God, then and only then can they drink from the Fountain of Signs and wonders.

Instead, they seek only the gifts of the fountains of God, and not God himself. They are unwilling to eat the fruits that God provides. It was the same in my time, people coming for the healings and signs and wonders, and not for a deeply intimate relationship with God."

I sadly agreed, "Even today, that many of God's people are the same way. They seek the gifts and experiences and not the giver of the gifts."

THE MOUNTAINS OF REFRESHING

John speaks again, "And seeking the gifts and experiences only; they will never become what God has called them to be on earth. You are called, as you know, to teach God's people who they truly are in Him.

Take what you learn and have learned and teach it to the people. All that you experience here is not just for you but for all God's people. God desires for all to have an intimate relationship with Him. Now it is time for you go, follow the path up the mountain."

With this, we say our goodbyes, and I continued up the path of one of the Mountains of Refreshing, I look back, to give the last wave goodbye to John, I see that he has already returned to his position sitting on the edge of the Foundation of Signs and wonders. I also saw some else lying on the ground, glowing with the power of the Holy Spirit. My curiosity wants to go back down the mountain and see who it is, but the Spirit is urging me to move on.

THE MOUNTAINS OF REFRESHING

As I turn and start up the mountain, I hear a roar off in the distance. The roaring was getting louder when suddenly I saw a great cloud of God's Glory racing towards me.

It's height and width is infinite (as far as I can tell). The cloud quickly engulfs me, and find that the Cloud of Glory is more like the ocean than a cloud. I am soon off my feet and being carried along by the powerful currents flowing in the Glory of God.

I have the freedom to move this way and then back another way, like swimming and skydiving at the same time. The love and power I feel flowing all around me are amazing.

At this point, I feel like the currents are moving me downward and I soon see the ground coming up from below. I gently step on the ground and calmly walk up the mountain again.

The path winds upward and comes to a place on the side of the mountain where I can see the view. The beautiful panorama before me is breath taking. I see off in the distance, great mountains, going higher than the one I am standing.

THE MOUNTAINS OF REFRESHING

Some of the mountains are pure gold, others out of silver still others large diamonds, others like rubies and still others like sapphires all glistening in the sun and seemly giving off wave after wave of the Glory of God.

Then, I look down to the valley below and realize that it is the Valley of the Fountains of God stretched out before me. Forgive me for being a little slow; it is then that it dawns on me that the Glory had swept me up and me perhaps hundreds of miles up the mountain.

As I stand there trying to take it all in, I hear a familiar voice saying, "Have you been waiting for me?" I turned around, and there is Katherine Kuhlman with a beautiful warm smile and the Glory of God surrounding her. I am speechless.

She says to me, "You are right, the Glory of God and the Spirit have carried you up the mountain, but they will take you only as far as you are willing to go. I learned this long ago before I came here to be with the Father, in His house."

Then, I say, "But, we are outside not in His house."

THE MOUNTAINS OF REFRESHING

Katherine says, (in a lovingly beautiful way) "Stop thinking in human terms of a house, Father's house encompasses all that there is, in both the physical and spiritual realms and beyond. And before you ask, Yes Father's house even includes those places; the evil one thinks are his and yes there are realms beyond the physical and spiritual that you cannot even begin to understand, now.

Learn as much as you can about the Father's Love. Learn how to express your love for him in all you do. Let him teach you who you truly are and are called to be.

Then meditate on what you learn and spend time with God. Get to know Him; that is the secret to it all. Teach others to do the same."

Then Katherine gave me a loving hug, turned, walked away and was gone.

I hear the roar once again and see the Glory coming down the mountain toward me. I am again, caught up in the cloud or the tidal wave of the Glory of God. This time is different.

THE MOUNTAINS OF REFRESHING

I not only feel and see the glory all around but I feel it flowing inside of me as well. I feel myself racing up the mountain, to the next encounter. Before I realize it, I am down once again. Waiting for me is a woman. I sense that I somehow know her, but I do not recognize her. She has a great authority around her.

She begins to speak, "I am Aimee Semple McPherson, and there is not much time, the next wave is coming, so just listen. I preached living a holy life before God, and God blessed me with many signs and wonders in my day. Learn that holiness is not the outward things you say or do.

Holiness has been imparted to you, into your spirit by the Father; release the Holiness of God from within you, and it let flow out like a mighty river. Many have learned that the Love of God flows out of you and yet they try to impose Holiness from the outside. It is the same for God's Holiness just as it is with God's Love. God's Holiness is within you, given to you at salvation and it must release from within you, out to the world that so desperately needs it.

THE MOUNTAINS OF REFRESHING

Anything else is dirty self-righteousness that does no good and only causes harm and destruction. Release God's Holiness from within you. Now go."

With that, I am swept up again by the Glory of God. This time I feel myself becoming one with the Glory and Spirit of God, flowing together as one, yet separate. I can no more describe what is happening than I can the Trinity. The three being one yet distinct, flowing together as one, yet flowing separately.

I come to rest on the peak of the Mountain of Refreshing, I look, and all I see is mountain tops and other mountains reaching up skyward, and out of sight, I look down, and cannot even see the valley below. I have learned much, and there is much to meditate on, yet I feel totally and completely refreshed.

THE KEYS

THE KEYS

I felt it is important to let you know what the keys are to have visions and to walk in heavenly places. It is vital that you do not try and do this on your own but let the Holy Spirit lead. You must know the Word of God. You must love God. Then build a relationship with God.

The first key is to know the Word of God. The Holy Spirit will not do anything that violates the Word of God. The written word is the check and balance to the Spirit. Without the written word to guide us, we can fall into the trap of deception. Knowing the Word of God is more than just reading it. It's more than memorization of scriptures. Head knowledge is important. To understand the Word of God takes study, finding the meaning of a passage of scripture. Then meditate on the word. Meditation is thinking on something over and over. Letting it get deep down in your spirit, into your heart.

The Word of God becomes a spiritual warning system within you. It gives a check in your spirit when something is not right, do not ignore it. Listening will save you a lot of heartaches. It can be as simple as being unsure about a spiritual experience, whether it's a personal or a corporate experience.

THE KEYS

There is nothing wrong with testing the spirit to see if it lines up with the Word of God. But to be able to do this you must have the Word of God in your heart, and that comes through study and meditation.

The second key is Matthew 22:37. Let's set the stage. The Sadducees have come to Jesus; remember they keep trying trip him up. They are so upset with him. They couldn't see whom they were dealing with; they were so wrapped with tradition and the law and trying to fulfill the law, which we all know you can't do. They had lost sight of the love of God and the need to love for God. They were doing everything they could, but they had lost their love for God. The Law and their traditions had become more important than God.

Jesus put it point blank when they ask, "Teacher which is the greatest commandment in the Law." And Jesus replied, "To love the Lord your God with all your heart, with all your soul, and with all your mind." And we know the latter part; love your neighbor as yourself, all the Law and Prophets hang on these two commandments.

THE KEYS

In Practice, the Presence of God by Brother Lawrence (1614-1691), stated he did everything with the attitude of love towards God. He states that with the grace of God everything becomes easy. Then he goes on to say, "That many to do not advance in the Christian progress because they stick in penance and particular exercises while they neglect the love of God which is its end."

How many of us get so wrapped up in what we do, that we forget the love of God, of taking time with him. I must sing in the choir; I must go to do this or that. I need be here at such and such a time. We have all this stuff to do. Whether it's what we consider spiritual things or natural things, we get so busy doing the stuff we forget to take the time to love God. We know God loves us. Jesus is saying Love the Lord your God with all your heart, soul, and mind.

Brother Lawrence is saying we neglect the loving of God. What we are learning about the love of God and about Loving God is not a new thing. Everyone thinks that soaking prayer and spending time in His presence is a new thing.

THE KEYS

It's as old as Jesus. It changes the perspective on what happens when you do the stuff, not for the love of a man or your desires, but out of your love of God.

There are a lot of organizations and people that do things out of love for humanity. Many of these organizations started with a love of God and man, but they forgot the key. The real key for everything we do is to do it out of our love of God.

Whether you are in Wal-Mart buying chicken for dinner, whether you are home being with your spouse or your children, whatever you do, do everything out of your love for God.

Loving God is the underpinning key for every one of the Giftings of the Holy Spirit to operate. We say, "We don't need to seek the gifts but to seek the giver." But more importantly than seeking the giver is to love the giver. Spending time in His presence is the key to loving God.

I know a lot of people say, "I don't have time to spend with God. I have my devotion in the morning, and then I have to prepare breakfast. I have to get the kids out the door.

THE KEYS

I have to go to work; I must to cut the grass, watch television, and play on the computer for a while."

What's important to you, you find time to do. If it does n't matter to you, it's a struggle to find time to do it. If it's important to you, you will find time to spend time with God and love Him. That's the beginning, everything we do we should do out of our love for God. Whether it's what we call natural things or spiritual things we should do them out of our love for God. It is out of love that we see things happen. As we love him, God pours out more than we can contain.

When we love him in everything, we do. God responds by pouring out His love into us, and all that He is and has is available to us. God says, "I love you so much, here it is." Taking time to be with God is not just doing Bible study or reading through the Bible in a year. Those things are important because you gain knowledge of the Word of God.

THE KEYS

God's word says, "Because he has set his love upon Me, therefore will I deliver him; I will set him on high, because he knows and understands My name [has a personal knowledge of My mercy, love, and kindness--trusts and relies on Me, knowing I will never forsake him, no, never]. He shall call upon Me, and I will answer him; I will be with him in trouble, I will deliver him and honor him. With long life will I satisfy him and show him My salvation." Psalm 91:14-16 (Amplified Bible).

We know this as the Psalm of God's protection. We all like declaring God's protection for us, but it is easy to forget the keys to this protection. The first key is that our will is involved; we decide to agree with the Lord and make Him our refuge and our dwelling place then the psalmist says we gain the Lord's protection.

Then God responds in verse 14 "because he has set his love upon me, therefore, will I deliver him…" God's essential is our love for him and having a personal knowledge of him. When we decide as an act of our will to love the Lord and know him personally, then we gain the protection that we so quickly declare.

THE KEYS

The third key is to know God, having a personal knowledge of him. Many people would say I love God because I know him. To a certain point, this is true, most believers have a basic knowledge of God and love him but what I am talking about goes much deeper.

An example of this can is marriage. When I started dating my wife in September 1978, I already knew her; we attended the same church, sang in the choir, were on the worship team, traveled and ministered as part of a young adult ministry team up and down the east coast. So, you can say I knew her. As we dated, I started learning more about her and love grew. After a time, I asked her to marry me, (thankfully she said yes) and we got married in August 1979. I knew and loved my wife. Since that time, I have grown in my love and knowledge of her, her likes and dislikes, the way she does things and even what buttons to push and not to push. So my knowledge as well as my love as grown and continues to grow since we first met.

That's how our relationship with God is to be. We start by knowing about God. It then moves to learning more and beginning to love him.

THE KEYS

This knowing brings to the point of salvation (example: the wedding) and the honeymoon (the Baptism in the Holy Spirit). Sadly, many believers stop right there and settle into their lives, and they stop growing in their knowledge and love of God.

After a few years, like many marriages, without increasing knowledge and love of each other, their relationship with God becomes boring and dull. Many people walk away from God looking for something new and exciting. Still, others stay in their "normal Christian life" expecting nothing more than what they already have.

But God wants us to know him more; He desires to reveal himself to us every day. Jesus said, "I came that they may have and enjoy life, and have it in abundance (to the full, till it overflows)" (John 10:10 Amp.).

This relationship is a far cry from "the normal Christianity" that many accept. We can know God in a personal, intimate relationship. We can learn something new and exciting about God, daily, but to do this, we must be willing to spend time with him and listen to him.

THE KEYS

It is out of spending time with God and desiring to know him more, that these visions came. Not from the desire of having visions. A growing, intimate relationship is the key.

I just determined to know God more. I spend time with him. Tit takes discipline, making an appointment with God and keeping it. It takes saying, "Father I want to spend time with you, come and be with me." Then sit quietly and wait to hear from him. Sometimes, I listen to instrumental worship music, other times I just sit and wait. Then like Adam and Eve, I look to the Father coming to spend time with me. Sometimes, it is just in His overwhelming presence, or He will speak to me, and still other times He gives visions.

I hope these keys are helpful to you. I pray that you will use them and enjoy your Adventures in the Spirit.

About the

Author

Richard L Spangler was born on July 14, 1955, in Norfolk, Virginia. He has lived in the Hampton Roads Area of Virginia his entire life. Richard came to know Jesus in August of 1969 and Baptized in the Holy Spirit in November of 1969.

Richard is an ordained minister and has been in active ministry since 1977. He has served as an assistant pastor and pastor. He is a Prophet and Teacher with a strong healing anointing. He has ministered in most of the east coast states and as far west as Texas.

He teaches believers the importance of having an intimate relationship with God and how to move in the Spiritual Giftings of the Holy Spirit. He also facilitates Spiritual Gifts Seminars and Leadership Training Seminars. He writes a blog and has written devotions for CBN.com.

Richard L Spangler is the founder of Lion's Voice Ministries. He is co-founder and administrator of the Mid-Atlantic Region Intercessory Prayer Network on Facebook. He has worked for the Christian Broadcasting Network (CBN) since August 2004.

He married his wife Dorthy, August 11, 1979, at the Rock Church in Virginia Beach Virginia. They have two beautiful daughters Mary and Sarah and a Granddaughter Parker Joy.

For articles by Richard L Spangler go to:lionsvoiceministries.blogspot.com

Send Richard your Comments to:lionsvoiceministries@yahoo.com

www.ingramcontent.com/pod-product-compliance
Lightning Source LLC
Chambersburg PA
CBHW070524030426
42337CB00016B/2090